:45 A.M. PEOPLE RACE UP OUT of the subway. They carry newspapers and briefcases. Some hold a small brown bag with a cup of coffee and bagel inside. Determined, they weave in and out of the sidewalk crowd on their way to work. Another morning starts on Wall Street.

★ ★ ★ ★

Less than 1 mile (1.6 kilometers) long, Wall Street runs between Broadway and the East River on the southern tip of Manhattan. Dwarfed by the skyscrapers that tower over it, this small street does not appear to be that special. However, Wall Street is the heart of New York City's **financial district**, a district so important it is also the financial center of the United States, if not the world.

It is hard to imagine that once there were no crowded streets, skyscrapers, or subways in lower Manhattan. However, before the Europeans came, Manhattan was an island of forests where woodland animals roamed and Native Americans traveled on trails hundreds of years old.

NEW AMSTERDAM

When the Dutch settled on Manhattan in 1625, they cleared the land and built small Dutch style houses. To honor the major city in their home country, the Netherlands, they named the settlement New Amsterdam.

Sponsored by the Dutch West India Company, the new settlers came to trade with the local Native Americans, the Munsees. They traded cloth, glass beads, and iron tools for food, furs, and "wampum," the blue and white shells that Native Americans used as **currency**, or money. The Dutch were particularly interested in the beaver, bear, and fox skins. Popular with Europeans, the furs made money for the colony.

Wall Street

CORNERSTONES
OF FREEDOM™

SECOND SERIES

Melissa Whitcraft

Children's Press®
A Division of Scholastic Inc.
New York • Toronto • London • Auckland • Sydney
Mexico City • New Delhi • Hong Kong
Danbury, Connecticut

Photographs © 2003: AP/Wide World Photos: 40 (Stuart Ramson), 37,
45 bottom (Amy Sancetta); Bridgeman Art Library International Ltd.,
London/New York/Private Collection: 11, 44 top left; Brown Brothers: 19,
22, 29, 44 bottom; Corbis Images: 3, 41 (AFP), 13, 18 top, 33, 36,
44 top right, 45 center (Bettmann), 34 (Jean Miele), cover top (Premium
Stock), cover bottom (RM), 38 (Alan Schein Photography, Inc.);
Hulton|Archive/Getty Images: 7, 8, 9, 10, 16, 23, 30, 45 top; North
Wind Picture Archives: 18 bottom, 5, 20, 21, 25, 27; Photo Researchers,
NY/LOC/SS: 17; Stock Montage, Inc.: 14, 31; Superstock, Inc./National
Portrait Gallery, London: 6; The Image Works/Topham: 24.

Library of Congress Cataloging-in-Publication Data
Whitcraft, Melissa.
   Wall Street / Melissa Whitcraft.
       p. cm. — (Cornerstones of freedom. Second series)
   Summary: Discusses the history and present role of Wall Street, the site
of the New York Stock Exchange as well as powerful brokerage houses
and investment firms. Includes bibliographical references and index.
   Includes bibliographical references and index.
   ISBN 0-516-24217-2
   1. Wall Street—Juvenile literature. 2. Stock exchanges—United
States—Juvenile literature. 3. Investments—United States—Juvenile
literature. 4. Stocks—United States—Juvenile literature. [1. Wall Street.
2. Stock exchanges. 3. Investments. 4. Stocks.] I. Title. II. Series: Cornerstones of freedom. Second series.
HG4572.W448 2003
332.64'273—dc21
                                                        2003005634

CHILDREN'S PRESS, and CORNERSTONES OF FREEDOM™, and
associated logos are trademarks and or registered trademarks of Scholastic
Library Publishing. SCHOLASTIC and associated logos are trademarks and
or registered trademarks of Scholastic Inc.

1 2 3 4 5 6 7 8 9 10 R 12 11 10 09 08 07 06 05 04 03

According to legend, in 1626 the Dutch "bought" Manhattan from the Munsees for goods worth $24. A nineteenth century historian came up with that price. It represented the value of the goods in the mid-1800s. Since Native Americans did not believe in selling land, it is doubtful the Munsees turned Manhattan over for any amount of money.

"DE WAL"

In 1653, When Peter Stuyvesant was governor, the Dutch built a 12-foot-high (3.7-m) wooden stockade across the northern section of the colony. Called "de wal," or "the wall,"

THE FIRST PEOPLE

When the Dutch arrived, Manhattan was inhabited by the Munsees. The Munsees were part of a large Native American group known as the Delaware. Both tribes spoke Algonquian. "Manhattan" comes from the Delaware-Algonquian word meaning "hilly island."

Dutch settlers built the Palisades in order to protect New Amsterdam against the British. The logs were 12 feet high and 18 inches thick, and the wall stretched from the East River to the Hudson.

Charles II is remembered as the handsome, good-natured, and fun-loving king of England who reigned from 1660 to 1685. Charles often gladly rewarded his friends among the nobility with land in North America.

the structure ran from the East River to the Hudson River. It protected New Amsterdam from both the local Native Americans and the British.

The wall, however, could not protect the Dutch from the English when they came by sea. In 1664 they arrived in New York harbor on four warships that carried five hundred soldiers. King Charles had decided to increase England's North American holdings. Stuyvesant tried to get the Dutch to resist, but since they weren't happy with his leadership, they refused.

The English came ashore without incident, and renamed the colony New York after King Charles's brother, the Duke of York. Eventually the wall came down, but in 1685, they built Wall Street, which still runs parallel to where the original structure once stood.

NEW YORK

New York became one of England's most prosperous colonies. By 1704 the British Royal Exchange was firmly established as a meeting place for **merchants** to trade such **commodities** as wheat, tobacco, and cotton. Occasionally slaves were traded as well. There was no reason to think that England would ever lose its hold on this profitable settlement.

However, King George III taxed the colonies unfairly. One of his most outrageous schemes

This notice appeared in a newspaper to advertise the sale of slaves. The first African Americans in New York did not arrive as slaves but as indentured servants who could gain their freedom after paying for their trip to the colonies through labor.

TO BE SOLD on board the Ship *Bance-Island*, on tuesday the 6th of *May* next, at *Ashley-Ferry*; a choice cargo of about 250 fine healthy NEGROES, just arrived from the Windward & Rice Coast. —The utmost care has already been taken, and shall be continued, to keep them free from the least danger of being infected with the SMALL-POX, no boat having been on board, and all other communication with people from *Charles-Town* prevented. *Austin, Laurens, & Appleby.*

N. B. Full one Half of the above Negroes have had the SMALL-POX in their own Country.

On July 9, 1776, impassioned New Yorkers gathered in Bowling Green Park at the southern tip of Manhattan and tore down the statue of King George III.

was the Stamp Act of 1765. The Stamp Act demanded colonists pay a tax for all newspapers, legal documents, and even playing cards they used. In October, colonial representatives met in New York to discuss ways to protest this tax on printed paper. Eventually the act was repealed, but there would be no stopping the drive for independence.

Fire broke out on the southern tip of Manhattan on September 21, 1776. It soon moved up to Wall Street and destroyed about 500 houses. It is suspected that Patriots set the fire before surrendering the city to the British.

On July 4, 1776, the Continental Congress in Philadelphia signed the Declaration of Independence. When the Declaration was read in New York on July 9, a mob pulled down a lead statue of King George III. They planned to melt the lead into bullets for the battles to come.

Once the British were finally defeated, New York was chosen as the country's first capital, and Federal Hall became the seat of the new government. There, on April 30, 1789, on a balcony overlooking Wall Street, George Washington was sworn in as the country's first president.

A NEW MARKET

New York was the new country's top commercial city. Much of its success was due to its geography. Situated halfway between New England to the north and the Chesapeake Bay to the south, New York was the perfect midway point for trans-Atlantic ships that traveled up and down the North American coast. In addition, New York City's large natural harbor protected ships during severe weather.

Federal Hall, pictured here around 1797, is where George Washington took his oath of office and made his first inaugural address on April 30, 1789.

A depiction of New York City's bustling waterfront as it may have looked in the 18th century.

As more products moved through New York, more merchants followed. During colonial times most trading was done by people who worked either for the king or for organizations such as the Dutch West India Company. With independence, individuals came to the city to make money for themselves. For the most part these merchants traded goods. However, a new market began to surface. In a limited way, traders started to buy and sell **securities**, such as **stocks** and **bonds**.

PAYING FOR THE REVOLUTION

To pay for the war against the British, the colonial government borrowed millions of dollars from both wealthy colonists and rich Europeans who supported the American cause. One colonial businessman who helped finance the revolution was Robert Morris. Morris, who signed the Declaration of Independence, would later establish the Bank of the United States. To pay back all these early financial supporters, in 1790 the new federal government sold $80 million in bonds to individuals who were willing to invest their money in this new nation.

★　★　★　★

Initially only bonds were traded. Bonds are loans. When a company or government needs to borrow money, it sells bonds to **investors**. These bonds promise to pay the money back within a certain amount of time. They also pay the investors additional money. This extra money is called interest. The interest on bonds is how the investor makes money.

The first stocks sold were bank stocks. Investors buy stocks, or shares in a company, to become shareholders, or part owners in that company. Shareholders hope that the company they have invested in will make money. If it does, their stock goes up in value. They can then make a **profit** by selling the stock. If a company fails, its stocks go down in value and the shareholder loses money.

THE BUTTONWOOD AGREEMENT

In the early 1790s all trading in New York was done outside. Merchants roamed up and down Wall Street, buying and selling goods and a few securities. There were no regulations. Prices went up and down in the time it took for a trader to cross the street and make a deal.

This confusion changed on May 17, 1792, when twenty-four merchants met under a buttonwood tree on Wall Street. Here they agreed to form a private trading group that would "give preference to each other in (its negotiations." These traders also agreed that they would make the same commission, or fee, on trades.

Known as the Buttonwood Agreement, this pact launched the first formal stock exchange in New York. A stock exchange is a trading market where traders, or stockbrokers, buy and sell securities for themselves and customers.

THE NEW YORK STOCK EXCHANGE

Today, New York's first formal exchange is called the New York Stock Exchange, or NYSE. In May, 2003, 84 million private investors and more than 300 brokerage firms owned shares in 2,800 companies listed on NYSE. These shares were worth more than $13.5 trillion at that time.

Meeting under a buttonwood tree, twenty-four stockbrokers established New York City's first official investment organization on May 17, 1792.

THE ERIE CANAL

The Buttonwood Agreement helped establish the financial markets of Wall Street. However, the success of these markets was still dependent on the success of New York as a

DeWitt Clinton, governor of New York, symbolically joined Lake Erie and the Hudson River in a ceremony that opened the Erie Canal on November 4, 1825.

port. When the Erie Canal was built, it guaranteed that New York would continue to flourish as a commercial center.

Begun in 1817 and finished in 1825, the Erie Canal was 350 miles (563 km) long and connected the Hudson River with Lake Erie. DeWitt Clinton, the governor of New York, fought for the canal because he knew it would speed up the flow of goods between the Midwest and New York. To finance the project, Clinton created New York State Bonds. The bonds were actively traded on Wall Street because investors also realized the canal was a good idea.

Clinton was on the first trip down the canal. When he arrived in New York harbor, he poured a barrel of Lake Erie water into the ocean. The act symbolized that the two bodies of water were one. The act also symbolized that Midwestern and Eastern markets were now one. No longer would the business of commerce be delayed by time-consuming trips over land.

PASSING THE WORD

To make money investors and traders need to buy and sell at a moment's notice. Stock prices have to be communicated as quickly as possible. In the early nineteenth century the New York and Philadelphia stock exchanges came up with an ingenious way to share information. They used flags. Men were stationed every 6–8 miles (10–13 km) between the two cities. Standing on hills or the roofs of buildings, each had a set of signal flags and a telescope.

When the market opened in New York, the first man used his flags to signal the prices of all the stocks being sold that morning. The next man, looking through his telescope,

Here is Wall Street, around 1847, looking west towards Trinity Church. Trinity Church was once the tallest building in Manhattan.

wrote down the information. Then, using his flags, he passed the information on to the next man down the line. Approximately thirty minutes later the New York prices arrived in Philadelphia where traders decided what they wanted to buy or sell.

On Wall Street itself stock information was carried by runners. Messengers raced from brokerage houses, or trading firms, and the exchange carrying buy and sell orders.

Both these methods of communicating lasted until Samuel Morse invented the telegraph in 1838. Morse's machine sent electrical pulses over wires. These pulses were controlled by a metal key that tapped out words in a series of dots and dashes. Once businesses had telegraph machines, they no longer needed runners or flags.

The telegraph was only the first communication device to help Wall Street. For example, in 1866, the year after the Civil War ended, the transcontinental telegraph cable was laid on the floor of the Atlantic. This cable connected New York and London. Traders no longer had to wait for ships to sail across the ocean to find out what the stock market was doing in England.

TICKER TAPE

As important as the telegraph and transcontinental cable were, the most innovative invention was the stock ticker. Edward A. Calahan, a telegraph operator, invented the machine in 1867. Based on the telegraph, it allowed brokerage houses all over Wall Street to get the same information at the same time.

THE EXCHANGE TAKES A POSITION

When the Civil War began in 1861, the New York Stock Exchange refused to do business with the southern states that had seceded from the union. Only after the war ended in 1865 did they open their doors to them again.

Samuel Morse began experimenting with the possibility of sending messages by electronic currents while a professor of arts and design at New York University in 1835.

This is one of the earliest stock ticker machines, which revolutionized the speed in which stock prices were transmitted.

In the late 1800s, investors often hovered around ticker tape machines waiting for stock prices.

* * * *

Using a central machine at the stock exchange, a telegraph operator typed in the stocks and their prices. The information was telegraphed to stock tickers throughout the financial district. Each stock ticker then printed the data out onto a thin strip of paper called ticker tape. Finally, reading the strip, a clerk wrote the stocks and their prices onto a blackboard.

By the mid twentieth century Calahan's machine had been replaced by electronic displays. Specialized computer programs also stock the information across the bottom of computer monitors. Certain television channels do the same. However, as advanced as the technology gets, traders still say they are reading "the tape."

New Yorkers greeted General Douglas MacArthur with a ticker-tape parade during the Korean conflict in 1951.

The tradition of ticker tape also continues through ticker-tape parades. For over a hundred years, politicians, heroes, astronauts, and winning New York sports teams have been honored with processions up Lower Broadway. Traditionally office workers in the tall buildings above showered the parade with ticker tape. Now shredded computer paper is used. However, any paper that flutters down these days is still called ticker tape.

Alexander Graham Bell demonstrated his telephone before judges at the Centennial Exhibition in Philadelphia on June 25, 1876.

★ ★ ★ ★

THE INDUSTRIAL REVOLUTION

Technological advancements continued to support the growth of New York's financial markets throughout the nineteenth century. The invention of the telephone in 1878 increased the speed in which business was done even more than the stock ticker had. Trading was now a phone call away, and deals could be made without brokers leaving their desks.

Electric light also transformed the financial district when Grosvenor Porter Lowrey, a Wall Street lawyer, brought electricity to the city. Lowrey funded the project with money from Wall Street investors. He also worked closely with Thomas A. Edison, who had invented the light bulb when he discovered a way to change electrical current into light.

At the same time that Wall Street was embracing these new inventions, the country was going through a period of great economic growth. Much of this growth came from the change in how Americans produced merchandise.

Before the nineteenth century, products were made by hand. By the mid 1800s machines had revolutionized production and did the work in less time and for less money than individual workers. This change, known as the

Industrial Revolution, created great wealth for the businessmen who owned the factories where the goods were made.

Between the 1840s and the 1890s, the growth of the country's railroad system also created great wealth for individuals and an economic **boom** for the nation as a whole. Railroads made it possible for factory-made goods to reach consumers throughout the United States. In addition, once rail travel reached the West Coast, easterners started moving west in greater numbers. Because the government encouraged this western settlement, it gave free land to businessmen who built the railroads. These businessmen then established successful transportation companies. Throughout this period jobs were plentiful. In factories, workers forged tracks and built passenger cars and engines. Engineers ran trains. Conductors sold tickets. Stations sprang up in small towns and large cities. However, while many people made some money during the boom, no one prospered more than the businessmen/investors who established the railroad companies.

Panic spread on Wall Street, Wednesday morning, May 14, 1884, due to the sudden failure of the Grant and Wood Bank. The panic proved not too serious, and business soon returned to normal.

THE ROBBER BARONS

The businessmen/investors of the transportation industry came to be known as the first of the Robber Barons. Robber

Andrew Carnegie rose from a life of poverty to become one of the shrewdest of the Robber Barons. In his later years, he became one of the most charitable of this elite and notorious group.

Barons built vast personal fortunes on and off Wall Street without giving much thought to those who got in their way. When necessary, some even bribed government officials.

One of the most famous Robber Barons was Andrew Carnegie. Carnegie built the American steel industry. In 1873 he started a mill in Pittsburgh that produced steel more efficiently and less expensively than it had been produced in the past.

Carnegie made a fortune with his steel mill and other businesses. Later in life he gave away his money. Regretting his earlier greed that ignored the rights of his workers, he said, "The man who dies rich, dies disgraced."

In 1901 Carnegie sold his steel mill to another Robber Baron, J.P. Morgan. Morgan ran the House of Morgan Bank. In addition to Carnegie's steel company, which became the U.S. Steel Corporation, Morgan controlled railroads, shipping lines, and electrical power plants. At one point this extraordinary **entrepreneur** had so much money he loaned the federal government $62 million to pay its bills.

A third **tycoon** of the time was John D. Rockefeller. He made his fortune in petroleum. In 1865 he built processing plants that refined the petroleum he pumped out of the ground into oil. Before the invention of the gasoline engine, petroleum was mostly in demand as kerosene, or lamp fuel, and as a lubricant for machinery. By 1879 Rockefeller's Standard Oil Company controlled 90%

Here is Wall Street as it looked around 1910.

John D. Rockefeller started the Standard Oil Company. Standard Oil's control of the oil industry made it a target in the fight to regulate monopoly power.

of the petroleum industry. This **monopoly** meant that Rockefeller controlled the price of oil. He could charge whatever he wanted because his was the only company that had oil to sell.

WHEELING AND DEALING ON WALL STREET

Most Robber Barons made their initial fortunes outside of Wall Street. However, they increased their wealth and influenced how stocks did by investing in the stock market. There was another group that also influenced how the financial markets did. These investors were called **speculators**.

Two of the more infamous, or notorious, speculators were Jay Gould and James Fisk. In 1869 they attempted to corner, or control, the gold market. They bought all the gold shares they could get their hands on. Their plan was to create a monopoly and then sell off the shares at a much higher price than what they had paid.

James Fisk and Jay Gould attempted to escape by ferry to New Jersey after their scheme to corner the gold market wreaked havoc on Wall Street.

When other investors realized what was happening, they too bought gold. Everyone wanted in on the deal. Suddenly gold shares were the most valuable stocks to own. Their price spiraled upwards. Eventually, the president of the United States, Ulysses S. Grant, realized what the two men were doing and demanded they stop. Their control of the gold market could have thrown the country into a **recession**, or economic decline.

On September 24, the stock market opened in a panic. Realizing that gold shares were not going any higher, traders started to sell. Gold prices fell. To stop the panic and stabilize the market, President Grant ordered the U.S. Treasury to release $4 million of its gold shares into the market.

When the gold panic was over, investors who lost money were furious. But no one was punished. No regulations were put in place to stop speculators from attempting such a plot in the future. It would take a much larger financial disaster before federal laws were passed to protect investors from the schemes of others.

OTHER EXCHANGES

Additional exchanges on Wall Street include the gold market, the commodities market, and the American Stock Exchange. The American Stock Exchange was originally known as the New York City Curb Exchange.

WHAT GOES UP MUST COME DOWN

At the start of the twentieth century the United States was a strong industrial nation, and new immigrants were arriving by the thousands to build their futures on the promise of a better life. In this positive environment, Wall Street thrived.

WORLD WAR I

The first major war of the modern era, World War I, was fought between two rival alliances. One group, the Central Powers, joined Austria, Germany, and the Ottoman-Turkish Empire. The other group, the Allies, united Britain, France, Russia, and the United States. The "Great War" was the culmination of years of tension between Europe's super powers.

"Curbstoners" were stockbrokers who traded securities on the street curbs in lower Manhattan. In 1921, they moved inside. In 1953 this Curb Market became known as the American Stock Exchange.

However, just as the stock market tends to do well when the business economy is flourishing, it tends to falter when events are unsettling. When World War I broke out in Europe in 1914, Wall Street investors were very concerned.

The conflict negatively affected international communications and trade. Investors began selling their stocks before they lost all their value. To stop the panic, the NYSE closed on July 31. It would not reopen for four and a half months.

The United States entered the war in 1917, and fought together with the Allies. In 1918 the Allies won and the war ended. By then the European nations were in shambles. Fighting the war had cost a great deal in terms of both money spent and lives lost. The United States, however, was still financially sound.

Because of this strength the center of the world financial market transferred from London to New York. Over the next ten years, a number of foreign companies would be listed on the New York exchange, and the American dollar would replace the English pound as the currency used in international markets.

Known as the "Roaring 20s," the decade after the war in the United States was one in which anything and everything was possible. Business boomed. The future looked bright. There was still poverty, particularly among immigrants and factory workers, but there were also more wealthy people than ever before, people who wanted to invest on Wall Street.

By 1928 stock prices were rising so high many investors believed they could not lose money. Filled with confidence they bought their stocks on **margin**. Buying on margin meant that if an investor wanted to buy $100 worth of stock he would pay only a fraction or small percentage of the actual cost of the stock, and borrow the rest. The loan would have to be paid back when the stock was sold. The investor gambled that, before the stock was sold, the shares would go up in value. Then, he could sell the stock, pay back what he owed, and pocket the profit.

THE CRASH

By the fall of 1929 the good times were over. Investors no longer trusted stocks to continue to rise. They panicked. Stocks slid. People who had bought on margin were caught.

The headline in the *New York Times* on the morning of October 29, 1929, announced the collapse of the stock market, marking the beginning of the Great Depression.

OTHER CRASHES

On October 19, 1987, the market went down over 22% in one day. People compared the event to the Crash of 1929. However, in 1987, new laws and procedures were in place to limit the immediate economic damage, and a crash was avoided.

Their shares were now worth less than their original value. This loss meant that many investors didn't have the money to pay back what they had borrowed to buy the stocks in the first place. All over the country people scrambled to get their money out of the market.

Sell orders flooded the exchange. On Tuesday, October 29, over sixteen million shares were traded, and approximately $14 billion of stock value was lost. The stock market "crashed," leading to a disastrous overall decline in the U.S. **economy**.

Fortunes vanished. Companies went under. Others saw the value of their stocks plummet. The Radio Corporation of America, RCA, was one. On September 3, RCA stock sold for $505 a share. By November 13, RCA stock had fallen to $28 a share. If you owned 100 shares you lost $47,700.

Crowds gathered on Black Tuesday, October 29, 1929, along Wall Street. Stocks fell in total value that day by more than $14 billion. By comparison, the U.S. government's entire annual budget at the time was only $3 billion.

30

During the Great Depression, President Franklin D. Roosevelt used radio programs known as "fireside chats" as a way to restore Americans' faith in their economic and political system. The only four-term president, Roosevelt led the United States through the Depression and to victory in World War II.

Banks failed as well. Many had lent money to investors who could not pay back their loans. Therefore, people who put their money into the banks were now bankrupt too. Home mortgages could not be paid. Businessmen could not pay their employees. By 1932 the economy was in such terrible shape that around twelve million people were out of work. The country was in the middle of the **Great Depression**.

THE NEW DEAL AND WORLD WAR II

In March 1933, Franklin Delano Roosevelt was elected President because he promised "a new deal for the American people." Immediately he started working with Congress to get the country's economy moving again. Two laws were passed that directly affected Wall Street.

One law was the Securities Exchange Act of 1934, which created the Securities and Exchange Commission, or SEC. The SEC oversees the sale of securities to protect investors. The second act created the Federal Deposit Insurance Corporation, or FDIC. FDIC guarantees that the federal government will pay the money owed to customers, up to a certain amount, if a bank closes for lack of funds. Other new legislation strictly regulated margin investing.

It took almost ten years for Roosevelt's New Deal to turn the country's economy around. However, companies did start up again. Factories reopened. People went back to work. Preparing for war helped.

When World War II broke out in Europe in 1939, the United States did not take part. Nevertheless, expecting that the time might come, factories built planes, trucks, tanks, and bombs. More people were put to work. At the Brooklyn Navy Yard, across the East River from Wall Street, over 70,000 workers were employed building warships and cargo carriers.

After the Japanese attacked the American naval base at Pearl Harbor on December 7, 1941, the United States did go to war. The country joined the Allied nations of England, France, and Russia to fight the Axis countries of Germany, Italy, and Japan. However, the stock exchange did not close, the way it had in World War I. Prepared for panic, there was none.

The first female stockbroker on Wall Street was Victoria Woodhull. Born in Ohio in 1838, Woodhull was quite controversial and progressive in her day. An immense success on Wall Street, Woodhull once said, "a woman's ability to earn money is better protection from the tyranny and brutality of men than her ability to vote." She also ran for president of the United States in 1872, many decades before women were even allowed to vote!

When the Allies won in 1945, Europe was once more in terrible economic shape. On the other hand, the economy in the United States was stable, and Wall Street's position as a world financial center was stronger than ever.

WALL STREET CHANGES

Historically, only white men ran the financial markets and brokerage houses of Wall Street. However, the second half of the twentieth century brought many changes. In 1967

A long way from ticker tape, the Nasdaq board displays the latest rises and drops in the market for the modern-day investor.

Muriel Siebert became the first woman to have a seat, or membership, on the New York Stock Exchange. In 1970 Joseph L. Searles III became the first African-American member. Today, the all white male institutions of the past no longer exist on Wall Street.

Financial institutions also began to advertise for customers. Television and print advertisements promised that people who invested their money with them would earn enough profit for college tuitions or second homes in the mountains. Now, it is more common than ever before for average Americans to have investments on Wall Street.

The second half of the twentieth century also brought more foreign investment firms to the financial district. In addition, Wall Street firms set up more offices in cities throughout the world. Computers, high speed Internet access, fax machines, and cell phones made it possible for brokers to trade around the world twenty-four hours a day. Wall Street was now truly global.

WALL STREET RISES HIGH

As Wall Street's importance as a global center increased, firms realized that to keep companies in the financial district new buildings had to be built. To help revitalize the area in the mid 1950s David Rockefeller, the grandson of John D. Rockefeller, decided to build an office tower in lower Manhattan for the Chase Manhattan Bank.

The Chase Manhattan Bank building was built, but the focus for this revitalized area became a building complex known as the World Trade Center (WTC). Designed by the Japanese American architect, Minoru Yamasaki, the twin towers of the WTC transformed the New York skyline and added ten million square feet (929,000 sq m) of office space to the financial district. When completed in 1973 each tower had 110 floors. The first tower was 1,305 feet (411 m); the second, 1,362 (415 m).

More skyscrapers rose up to join the World Trade Center. This burst of construction reflected the success Wall Street

The construction of the World Trade Center began in 1966 and both towers were completed by 1973. The towers were designed to be able to withstand the high winds and storms that blow into New York City.

was enjoying. The last two decades of the twentieth century had been a period of unprecedented economic growth for the United States. Investment brokers around the world were looking forward to the new millennium.

SEPTEMBER 11, 2001

Shortly before nine on September 11, 2001, a hijacked American Airlines jet flew into the North Tower of the World Trade Center. Less than twenty minutes later a hijacked United Airlines plane crashed into the South Tower. Within two hours the twin towers had collapsed in a roar of bent steel, concrete, and glass.

New Yorkers fled lower Manhattan on September 11, 2001, as the South Tower of the World Trade Center collapsed after the terrorist attack.

37

The New York Stock Exchange proudly showed its patriotism after September 11, 2001. The flag also symbolized Wall Street's resilience following the attacks on America's other symbol of economic power—the World Trade Center.

As the day went on it became apparent that the attack was part of a larger terrorist plot. Another hijacked plane crashed into the Pentagon, the headquarters for the Department of Defense, and a fourth plane, taken over by passengers, went down in the Pennsylvania countryside.

The hijackers were members of an extremist Islamic group called Al-Qaeda. Al-Qaeda members are violently anti-American because of U.S. policies in the Middle East. Al-Qaeda, however, was not the first terrorist group to attack the World Trade Center, the symbol of American financial power. In February 1993 another extremist Muslim group exploded a car bomb in one of the twin towers underground garages. In that attack 1,000 people were injured and six were killed.

Nearly 3,000 people were killed in the September 11, 2001, attack on the World Trade Center. The financial district was devastated. The stock exchange closed for four days while rescue workers dealt with the chaos. When the market reopened, investment firms from the World Trade towers and other destroyed buildings had lost more than their offices and records. In some cases hundreds of their employees had been killed.

THE FUTURE

Amid the destruction and despite the terrible sadness, business did go on. Displaced companies moved to temporary offices at other locations. Companies helped each other get back on their feet.

The attack hurt the economy. People lost jobs. Investors, nervous about the future, were not as quick to put money in the market. In the months after the attack, the discovery that several large corporations had lied about their profits also reduced investor confidence in Wall Street.

THE WAR ON TERRORISM

Seeking to close down Al-Qaeda and other terrorist organizations, the United States waged a "War on Terrorism." American troops, along with other nations, have shut down Al-Qaeda camps in Afghanistan. Individual terrorists have been captured in the Mideast, Europe, and the United States.

However, the terrorists failed to bring the U.S. economy to a halt. On September 8, 2002, members of Congress met in Federal Hall for the first time since 1790. They came to Wall Street, as New York Mayor Bloomberg said, to show the world "that the spirit of this city and the spirit of this country remain unshaken."

The Al-Qaeda destroyed two towering symbols of world finance, but they did not destroy global finance. They did not destroy Wall Street. The World Trade Center is gone, but cleared of debris, if not

Olympic figure skating gold medalist Sarah Hughes rang the opening bell at the New York Stock Exchange on Monday, March 4, 2002, after returning home to New York following the 2002 Winter Olympics.

memories, the site is ready for the future: a future in which new structures will rise, businesses will return, and a memorial will acknowledge what happened there.

The spirit of Wall Street is not unshaken. Monday through Friday people still race out of the subway, briefcases and coffee in hand, ready to do business. There will always be another morning on Wall Street.

Glossary

bond—a document written by a government or company that promises the money borrowed will be paid back, with interest, by a specific date

boom—period of rapid economic growth

commodities—unprocessed goods such as wheat, tobacco, and cotton

currency—form of money used as means of exchange

economy—the running of a country based on its production and use of goods

entrepreneur—a person who runs and takes responsibility for a business

financial district—an area which relates specifically to businesses such as banks, investment firms, and stock markets

Great Depression—an economic crisis started by the stock market crash of 1929

Industrial Revolution—period of change starting in the late eighteenth and early nineteenth centuries in which manufacturing shifted from individual hand-made products to machine-made factory merchandise

margin—money borrowed by an investor from a stockbroker that represents partial payment for a stock bought

merchant—a businessperson who buys and sells goods or products

monopoly—total control by a person or group in the manufacturing and selling of a product or service

profit—money received after all expenses have been paid in a business deal

recession—a time when business profits slow down

securities—certificates that confirm a person's ownership of stocks or bonds

speculator—a person who risks losing money to make a fortune

stocks—shares that represent partial ownership in a company

tycoon—a powerful businessperson

Timeline: Wall Street

1625
Dutch settle on Manhattan, name settlement New Amsterdam

1664
English take over Dutch colony, name it New York

1776
Declaration of Independence signed in Philadelphia

1789
George Washington sworn in as first President at Federal Hall

1792
The Buttonwood Agreement signed, creating New York's first stock exchange

1929
The stock market crashes after an uncontrollable day of selling

1929–1939
The Great Depression

1939–1945
World War II

1960s–1970s
Wall Street opens doors to minorities and women

1973
World Trade Center completed

1825

The Erie Canal completed. New York now connected to the Midwest

1830s

Industrial Revolution changes the way merchandise is produced

1867

Invention of the stock ticker by Edward A. Calahan

1869

The gold panic started by Jay Gould and James Fisk, Jr.

1889

The *Wall Street Journal* first published

1914–1918

World War I

1921

The New York City Curb Exchange moves inside, becomes the American Stock Exchange

2001

World Trade Center destroyed; War on Terrorism begins

2002

Congress returns to Federal Hall

45

To Find Out More

BOOKS

Bookbinder, Bernie. *City of the World: New York and its People.* A New York Newsday Book, Harry N. Abrams, Inc.: New York, 1989.

Buck, James E., Editor. *The New York Stock Exchange, The First 200 Years.* Greenwich Publishing Group, Inc.: CT, 1995.

Hakim, Joy. *A History of Us, Book Three: From Colonies to Country, Book Four: The New Nation, Book Seven: Reconstruction and Reform, Book Eight: An Age of Extremes, Book Nine: War, Peace, and All That Jazz.* Oxford University Press: New York, 1993.

WEBSITES

Robber Barons: Robber Barons, by J. Bradford deLong
http://econ161.berleley.edu/Econ_Articles/carnegie/delong_moscow_paper2.html

The History Channel.com
- Depressions
- Stock Exchange
- Securities and Exchange Commission
- Wall Street
http://www.historychannel.com

ARTICLES

"The Height of Ambition"; James Glanz & Eric Lipton, The New York Times Magazine, The New York Times, 9/08/02

Index

About the Author

Melissa Whitcraft lives in Montclair, New Jersey, with her husband and two sons. She has a Master of Arts in theater. In addition to plays and poetry, she has written both fiction and nonfiction for children. She has published *Tales From One Street Over*, a chapter book for young readers. Her biography, *Francis Scott Key, a Gentleman of Maryland*, was published as a Franklin Watts First Book. Ms. Whitcraft has written books on the Tigris and Euphrates, the Niagara, and the Hudson rivers for the Watts Library series. She also wrote *Seward's Folly* and *The Mayflower Compact* for the Cornerstones of Freedom, Second Series.